Sports and Activities

Let's Swim!

by Carol K. Lindeen

Consulting Editor: Gail Saunders-Smith, PhD

Consultant: Kymm Ballard, MA
Physical Education, Athletics, and Sports Medicine Consultant
North Carolina Department of Public Instruction

Capstone
press

Mankato, Minnesota

Pebble Plus is published by Capstone Press,
151 Good Counsel Drive, P.O. Box 669, Mankato, Minnesota 56002.
www.capstonepress.com

1 2 3 4 5 6 11 10 09 08 07 06

Library of Congress Cataloging-in-Publication Data
Lindeen, Carol K., 1976–
Let's swim! / by Carol K. Lindeen.
    p. cm. — (Pebble plus. Sports and activities)
    Includes bibliographical references and index.
    ISBN-13: 978-0-7368-5367-5 (hardcover)
    ISBN-10: 0-7368-5367-7 (hardcover)
    1. Swimming—Juvenile literature. I. Title. II. Series.
GV837.6.L56 2006
797.2—dc22   2005017595

Summary: Simple texts and photographs present the skills, equipment, and safety concerns of swimming.

Editorial Credits
Heather Adamson, editor; Kia Adams, designer; Kelly Garvin, photo researcher

Photo Credits
Capstone Press/TJ Thoraldson Digital Photography, cover, 1, 5, 9, 15, 19, 21
Getty Images/The Image Bank/Tracy Frankel, 17; Marina Jefferson, 7
Index Stock/Tom Carter, 13

Note to Parents and Teachers

The Sports and Activities set supports national physical education standards related
to recognizing movement forms and exhibiting a physically active lifestyle. This book
describes and illustrates swimming. The images support early readers in understanding
the text. The repetition of words and phrases helps early readers learn new words.
This book also introduces early readers to subject-specific vocabulary words, which are
defined in the Glossary section. Early readers may need assistance to read some words
and to use the Table of Contents, Glossary, Read More, Internet Sites, and Index sections
of the book.

Table of Contents

Swimming 4

Swimwear 14

Safety 16

Having Fun 20

Glossary 22

Read More 23

Internet Sites 23

Index 24

Swimming

Splish! Splash!

It is fun to swim

in the water with friends.

People swim in pools, lakes, and oceans.
Swimming areas usually have shallow and deep water.

Swimmers make strokes
through the water.
They kick their legs and
push and pull their arms.

Swimmers jump and dive

into deep water.

Then they swim back

to the edge.

Some swimmers like to race.

They may be part

of a swim team.

Swimwear

Swimmers wear swimsuits
or swim trunks.
They put on sunscreen
when they swim outdoors.

Safety

New swimmers take lessons.

Teachers explain safety rules.

They show swimmers how

to practice in shallow water.

Lifeguards watch swimmers
and keep them safe.
They make sure swimmers
follow the rules.

Having Fun

Come splash, jump, and dive.

Let's go swimming!

Glossary

lake—a body of water surrounded by land

ocean—a large body of salt water that covers a large part of the earth

shallow—not very deep

stroke—a pattern of arm and leg movement in swimming

sunscreen—a lotion or spray that protects skin from the sun; swimmers use waterproof sunscreen.

swimsuit—a one- or two-piece outfit made for swimming worn by girls and women

swim trunks—shorts made for swimming worn by boys and men

Read More

Crossingham, John, and Niki Walker. *Swimming in Action.* Sports in Action. New York: Crabtree Publishing, 2003.

Eckart, Edana. *I Can Swim.* Sports. New York: Children's Press, 2002.

Klingel, Cynthia, and Robert B. Noyed. *Swimming.* Wonder Books. Chanhassen, Minn.: Child's World, 2001.

Internet Sites

FactHound offers a safe, fun way to find Internet sites related to this book. All of the sites on FactHound have been researched by our staff.

Here's how:

1. Visit *www.facthound.com*

2. Type in this special code **0736853677** for age-appropriate sites. Or enter a search word related to this book for a more general search.

3. Click on the **Fetch It** button.

FactHound will fetch the best sites for you!

Index

deep, 6, 10

dive, 10, 20

jump, 10, 20

kick, 8

lakes, 6

lessons, 16

lifeguards, 18

oceans, 6

pools, 6

race, 12

rules, 16, 18

shallow, 6, 16

strokes, 8

sunscreen, 14

swimsuits, 14

swim team, 12

swim trunks, 14

Word Count: 123
Grade: 1
Early-Intervention Level: 14

14.95

03-29-06